COUNCIL OF
SELEUCIA CTESIPHON

Mar Joseph of Seleucia,
Catholicos of the Church of the East

Translated by: D.P. Curtin

Dalcassian
Publishing
Company

PHILADELPHIA, PA

Copyright @ 2014 Dalcassian Publishing Company

All rights reserved. No part of this publication may be reproduced, distributed, or transmitted in any form or by any means, including photocopying, recording, or other electronic or mechanical methods, without the prior written permission of the publisher, except in the case of brief quotations embodied in critical reviews and certain other non-commercial uses permitted by copyright law. For permission request, write to Dalcassian Publishing Company at dalcassianpublishing at gmail.com

ISBN: 979-8-8691-8536-5 (Paperback)

Library of Congress Control Number:
Author: Curtin, D.P. (1985-)

Printed by Ingram Content Group, 1 Ingram Blvd, La Vergne, Tennessee

First printing edition 2014.

SYNOD OF MAR JOSEPH, CATHOLICOS, AND EIGHT BISHOPS WHO WERE WITH HIM.

To the venerable friends of God, our brothers and colleagues, the metropolitans and bishops of the provinces of the Eastern region, who, in true joy to Christ, are in communion, by paternal restitution, with the apostolic throne, which is fixed in the Church of Koke, in the royal cities of Seleucia and Ctesiphon.

He who loves you and thirsts for your kind sight, Joseph, servant and minister of all, by the grace of God and by the participation and consent of all the bishops and archbishops, institute catholicos, patriarch, by the mercy of the Lord of all things; and your priests and friends the Jews of the great province of the apostolic, patriarchal and paternal see, established in the great church of Koke, in Seleucia and Ctesiphon, gathered with us:

Abundant peace in Christ, the hope of our life, which protects you from all harmful things.

The blessed apostle Paul, who is the schoolmaster of the divine mysteries, the doctor and paranymph of the bride of the celestial bridegroom, who is the holy

COUNCIL OF SELEUCIA-CTESIPHON

Church, instructs us by saying: "I have no difficulty in writing to you these things." Nor will we experience any difficulty in writing and in reminding Charity of the things which you know perfectly and of which you are convinced, all of you who, by the grace of Our Lord, are the doctors of God, chosen in his foreknowledge and accredited as the shepherds and leaders of the flocks of the sheepfold of Our Lord Jesus Christ, Son of the living God. — The reason which invites us at this moment to address these merits to you and to involve your Charity in common affairs is this:

In the year 863 of the count of the Greeks, according to the time of Alexander son of Philip, our predecessor, our Father of happy memory Mar Aba left this world. Because of the duality which had existed prior to his government and also because of the hatred of the pagans and the accusations of the Christians, which followed his accession to the leadership (of the Church). He had to undergo various imprisonments and exiles. This had enabled certain disruptors and corrupters to accomplish the design of their malice, to disturb proper order, to trample underfoot ecclesiastical canons and to despise divine precepts, to sow discord, that is to say, disturbances and divisions, and to provoke revokes. They have constituted themselves, of their own will, foreign to all fear of God. Those who called themselves from the house brought abominable accusations before the people outside against Mar Aba, Catholicos, our predecessor, of good memory, because he blamed them and addressed them with reprimands, so that they would return from their bad habits, that They convert to the Lord and do penance, so as to obtain mercy and not die in their sins. But the more this saint worked for them, the more they hardened and the more they aggravated the heavy weight of their crimes. Ended his days in bonds and received his reward from God, Lord of all things; he was an admirable example for all those everywhere who fear the name of the Lord.

In the year 863 (552 AD), in the month of Iyar, by the effect of the grace of God, by the choice and agreement of the entire community, I, a vile wretch, was clothed with the supreme priesthood, with blessed memory, with the empire the Persians, designed the east side of the Holy Church from the royal windows of Seleucia and Ctesipion. The assembled bishops then earnestly requested that, whenever occasion permitted, the canons of the Fathers be renewed, and as governed, the canons and ecclesiastical traditions be observed -

as before. But, as the moment was not favorable, we decided, at this time, to write to you.

In the year 864 bishops met and presented us again with a petition on the same subject. Urgent causes and business prevented us; and it seemed to us universally that it was useless to write before all the matters which presented difficulties had received a solution.

And after, by the grace and mercy of the Lord, these affairs had received a happy solution, the six bishops assembled again in 865, in the month of kanoun, for this purpose. They made earnest entreaties, suffering much and being afflicted unto death by the corruption and confusion which are in the holy Church of the East, and they addressed supplications to all the pastors, their brothers, saying: "The canons of the Fathers, thanks to which the true Church has grafted and is consistent in the love of God, as well as all the orders and all the classes, which are in them, have fallen into obsolescence, have been neglected, have disappeared from the memory of a great number, because of the disturbance introduced by Satan, by means of men carrying out their own will. And it is the same as if these canons had never existed or been established in Holy Elegance. Knowing that you are all shepherds willing and prepared like skilled boatmen and prudent pilots who, by their diligence, their knowledge and their wisdom, save their boats in the midst of the violent storms and the turbulent waves which rise against them on the humid and foaming inert, and lead them to the peaceful port, to a place of rest and security. We have written to you so that you also save the vessel of your Souls and the Souls which have been confined to you, of the storms that the Galomniator has excited against the Church by the hands of his deceitful disciples, who, through their egoism, have beaten Christianity through the profanation of the canons, the contempt for the observances and the laws of God. So that you guard your shepherds and your flocks against those who, clothing of sheep's skins, comes out drunk in it from the ravishing and destructive wolves; — so that we and you, all together, prepare, arrange and complete the things to which the grace of the Holy Spirit invites us, and these canons which are like raised walls, impregnable fortresses, protecting their guards against all danger, and like lamps illuminating those who await the mother of Christ. Those who wish to walk in the iron of the royal residence, leveled and cleared, walk there in safety, thanks to the canons defined by the 318 ecumenical Fathers by the operation of the Holy Spirit, and by the 150 Fathers gathered in Constantinople and by all the synods of the Fathers."

These canons, which unfortunately in our days have been forgotten, we have renewed and we renew them in this holy synod of our holy assembly, we, and we all; so that these canons which are Merit, in order, below, may be confirmed by us, by you, and by the whole community, by means of signatures and seals, under the sanction of the word of God.

Above all, we keep the orthodox confession of the two natures in Christ, that is to say of his divinity and his humanity; we keep the properties of natures and we repudiate in them any kind of confusion, disturbance, mutation or change. We also preserve the number of the three persons of the Trinity, and, in a single true and ineffable unity, we confess one true Son of one God, Father of truth. Whoever thinks or says that there are two Christs or two Sons, and for any reason or in any way introduces a quaternity, we have anathematized and re-anathematize, and we consider him a rejected member of the whole body of Christianity. Furthermore, we keep everything that is proper to the chaste and holy alliance; we will guard the ecclesiastical canons with vigilance and with more care than our own bodily lives. And whoever transgresses even one of the canons merits below will be liable to the penalty decreed by each of them.

Canon I. — It was said in the Synod that someone had come to ask to "be established priest in another province by the holy catholicos Mar Joseph. We answered him that the canons do not allow anyone to establish priests in that diocese, which is not his, especially a person about whom we had no insight to know whether he was worthy or not. He went to seek refuge among people outside, among the great ones of the kingdom. These in turn made pressing requests in his favor; but as it was not appropriate to accept this petition, because it constituted a transgression of the canons, it was not accepted. For this reason, this impious person went to incite these people, and, because of his accusations, the church of his village was destroyed, and people of the place were chained under the pretext that they and their fathers had recently spoken falsehoods. Those who were not robust were apostates. After a lot of damage was caused, the local bishop made great representations to a few people to persuade him to stop accusing Christians and to become a priest. By such a process of impiety this scoundrel received the formation of the priesthood, whereas he should have received the just punishment for his impiety. — This is why it seems good to us, if a deacon, a priest or a bishop seeks to secure a considerable place for himself under the patronage of people from outside or of the secular faithful, that he be deposed and removed from the order which he received. The faithful who have given him their assistance will also be deprived of any ecclesiastical participation, until they do penance. And if anyone thinks of imitating him in these or similar things, we advise him to cease this work immediately; and, if he does not obey, let him be deprived and stripped of the order he received, whoever! Either; and if, not having yet received the priesthood, he dares to originally meditate on iniquity, let him be excluded from all ecclesiastical participation and from all communion with the faithful, he and those who lend his hand, if they are faithful, until the fruits of penitence are seen in them.

Canon II. — It was said that in a certain place there were two churches in the same village: one which was called the new church, and the other the old church. And there was a separate assembly in each of the two. For any matter whatsoever, the bishop wrote a letter to the priests and the faithful of the assembly of the new church; those who belonged to the old church seized the letter, took it to the bishop and delivered it to the Persians. On the testimony of the bishop who called it "new", this church was destroyed; so that the whole assembly was united into one and the clerics could satisfy their greed. — This is why we canonically define that: Where there are two churches and two assembled, they will not use their neighbor to destroy the church and attract to them a community which was not dependent on them, by exposing the priests, their brothers, to the barracks, plunder of property and apostasy from Christianity. Those who act in this way will be rejected and deposed from all orders of the priesthood.

Canon III. — It has also been said that bishops take their seats from one another, thanks to the patronage of the faithful and people from outside, and that also, freely and voluntarily, they establish priests in each diocese. — This is why we canonically decree that: "We commit him who desires what does not belong to him to be content with what is his; that he does not hate the spirit who was betrothed to him by the Lord. We invite him there out of charity; If he does not listen, let him be excommunicated, and if, being excommunicated, he does not obey, let him be rejected and removed from all orders of the priesthood. As for those who follow the canons and make ordinations in a diocese which is not theirs: let the ordination be null and void; and if there is no reason which prevents the transgression of the canons, let the sentence be carried out as it was defined."

Canon IV. — It has also been said that in certain places, at the death of a priest, factions and coalitions were produced, each wanting to make his own feeling prevail; and, carried away by human passion, they share with the seculars the ardor of their convictions and associate clerics; and without the bishops of the province, without the assembly of all the clergy and the faithful, they enter into secret election of the person they desire. They also make oaths and pacts promising that until death they will not abandon this person. For this reason, they collect funds to make damages, for considerable events occur in the community. This is why we have defined that: "Those who act in this way will be forbidden and deprived of any participation in the life of the saints, and of any communication with the faithful. As for the person that agrees to this, if the thing was done without his knowledge, and he then gave him consent, he will be deprived of all ecclesiastical participation, as befits his fault. if, on the contrary, he himself, through his diligence and his care, led them to act in this way, and if he does not abandon this audacious feeling that he conceived, he will be rejected, deposed and destroyed, stripped of the rank he occupied.

Canon V. — It was said, in a synodal assembly of the bishops of the West, that anathema strikes anyone who leaves one seat for another. This anathema was despised: and the door was opened to fornication in the holy Church; wherever it took place, its results are not good, but it results from ruin, and considerable damages. Those done to the poor, which are not to be classified under the anathema of the Perisians in their canon, to distance this fornication from the Church of God, for the impure are not to be among the priesthood of the Lord Christ by His celestial authority. That it is not lawful for anyone to leave one seat for another. If anyone is quickly requested by the people inside, or by those outside, that he does not give in to their entreaties, but that he persists in the observance of the canons. That is to say in chaste accord with the spiritual woman which was given to him "Let him who dares to violate this definition be rejected and removed from all ranks of the priesthood. Let him also be deprived of all educational participation, until he does penance and the assembly of bishops judges it appropriate to do so." Do not grant him participation in the holy mysteries.

Canon VI. — It has also been said that there are certain bishops who, in the general assembly, do with good will everything that is presented to them by their superiors and their directors. For some time, some people have denied this saying: "We did not do it", others say: "We did it by constraint." It thus turns out that something else is their words and something else their actions. There are some who incite to put the delinquents on trial, then when the judgment is about to be pronounced and the penalty for their sins is announced in writing in the general assembly, where all the bishops gave mutual consent, they opposed what the assembly of bishops did. — Among these we must canonically say: "That a severe reprimand will be addressed to them by their brothers; and if they do not abandon their habits, let them be deprived of the functions of the priesthood. If they persist further in their audacity and do not obey the advice and opinion of their brothers, let them be given a fixed and limited time to correct themselves and without them being able to exercise their ministry, by the word of God. If their wound is not healed, let them be stripped and deprived of all priestly orders."

Canon VII. — He said that men raised to the degree of supreme paternity, that is to say, to the patriarchy, handle matters alone, finish them and sign them, and, without showing them to the bishops or reading them in their presence, imperiously demand that they sign them. And if they do not sign them, they cause trouble, anathematize them and reject them from the episcopate. — This is why we have defined that: "The metropolitan or the patriarch must do everything he does with the council of the church. The matter which he has settled will have all the more authority as it has been submitted to the examination of more numerous bishops. If the urgency of the matter does not allow time to bring together the bishops, or if the speed of the matter does not leave the necessary time, because it allowed him to persist until the arrival of the bishops, it resulted in certain damages, because of negligence, in these cases of authority, without the precedence of three bishops." Because the assembly of three bishops can be seen as an assembly of tents according to the word of our Lord who said: "Wherever there are two or three united as one, I will be in the midst of them", — Whoever dares to act unilaterally will be liable to sentence and penalty that the assembly deems appropriate.

Canon VIII. — It has been said that priests and superiors often abandoned their residences without the permission of the bishop and went to other places which they felt were richer than the first, which they had found flourishing at their installation, which was devastated over time and abandoned by others. — Concerning this we have defined canonically: "That we must no longer entrust them with the direction of churches or monastics. Everything which will be found belonging to churches or churches will be put back in its place. The bishop of the place will address them with the appropriate admonitions, and, if it is useful to do something else with regard to them, including the punishment of their privileges and their freedoms.

Canon IX. — It is said that certain priests, who have practiced iniquities and are accused by people within as well as those without, and have not shown sincere penitence, but only for the outward form and by necessity. They do this while the directors for certain reasons go over and give them permission to execute the ministry in their territory. And, instead of being touched by these miseries, they seek protection! Among people from within and without and they reach the episcopate. As they themselves have previously been blameworthy and guilty, they can no longer criticize and reprimand those in whom vices are found. — Concerning these we have defined canonically that. He who, being the teacher of others, has transgressed the canons and has done something contrary to Christian morals, even though he would have used mercy towards him, and would have been left in his first actions, he will not be able to achieve the dignity of fatherhood, which is the episcopacy. Those who transgress these things will be prohibited and deprived of their priestly ministry, until they do penance in the manner that will be prescribed for them by the assembly of bishops. Anyone who has received the episcopate will be rejected and dismissed from the order he received.

Canon X. — It has been said that priests, deacons, clerics will take pagan women and some of them converted and begot children from them. After a while, when the Magi learned of this, these women were seized, and they were chained up, and they abandoned Christianity. Certain priests or deacons are dishonored by their apostate children. — This is why we have definitively denounced that: Those who act in this way will no longer be admitted to exercise the priesthood."

Canon XI. — It has been said that there are among the bishops and priests to whom the registers of Church property are entrusted. Some monasteries, and the men who inhabit them, by writing them in their name and making themselves the author of their sons and their lilies. And sometimes they marry their wives or daughters, and inherit the property of churches and monasteries, which are not lost only for the churches and convents, but even for the entire Christian community! — This is why we have defined it canonically: "That those who are established in a community cannot make a will without the opinion and assembly of the community; and, if they make a will in secret, it will be broken and annulled by the ecclesiastical judge."

Canon XII. — He also said that among the bishops, priests, deacons, clerics or faithful, who have been, because of their faults, deprived, by the word of God, of priestly actions, or of the reception of holy mysteries, or of the communion of the faithful, there are some who accept, then seek a refuge near people outside to obtain their forgiveness by force, even before having consigned their vices. And if there is someone who opposes them and enforces the canons, these people have great power, which makes them suffer serious afflictions by royal chores, by worldly nonsense, and by all kinds of other means. There are others who do not accept their prohibition, pose as rebels, attract certain quarrelsome men to their side and form a party with the aim of deposing the bishop of the place and put in his place another who will do their will. — Concerning these people, we have defined canonically: "That they must be deprived of all ecclesiastical communion for a certain time. If they acknowledge their fault and do penance, they will be forgiven; but, on the contrary, they persist in their stubbornness, exciting all the more troubles and disputes as they are with the faithful; if they are faithful, let them be deprived of all communion. If they a convert, they will be allowed to receive the holy mysteries.

Canon XIII. — It has been said that there are reprehensible secularists who, because of their contempt for the canons, are not even worthy of the peace of the Church, and who nevertheless say that there is a synod, which has come to sit in the first place. While they are not even faithful to the precepts of Christianity, they make themselves judges of clerics, deacons, priests and even bishops. As for their own faults, they don't consider this! — Concerning these we have defined canonically: "That not only in the assembly of the community, they must not go up where the leader is, but that they are not even worthy of being given a seat in the general assembly, for any matter whatsoever. If they are summoned for a necessary cause, let them stand like guilty ones. If they want to be judged, let them first judge themselves, and then they will judge those who are better than themselves. And we have defined under the anathema that no one is permitted to act otherwise give more time for penance, if they do not agree to have pity on their souls, and to recover health through the forgiveness and resolution of the community. If they are priests, let them be rejected and dismissed from their ministry, deprived of any participation."

Canon XIV. — It was also said this: "When the Father of Fathers dies, that is to say the patriarch, so that the one chosen for the supreme priestly paternity is received with the consent of the whole community, it is appropriate that all the metropolitans must participate in an election." That is to say, either in writing or by the imposition of hands, if it is in time of peace and there is nothing to fear or dread in delaying the matter. If, on the contrary, times are troubled and agitated, made difficult for Christianity by people from outside, a leader and a director will be given promptly to the community, with the consent of two metropolitans, in fear that oppression and persecution against Christianity is not increased by those who are in opposition, and only the disruptors, who call themselves Christians do not find the opportunity to excite schisms and divisions, as happened in our old days. — This is why we have defined that: "When, with a right intention and a just design, without respect for anyone and without human passion, the clergy and the faithful of the two cities of Seleucia and Ctesiphon elect a leader, with the bishops of the province of this see, with the consent of two metropolitans. All the provinces must accept with joy and goodwill the one who has been established their leader and their director by the grace of the Holy Spirit. All bishops, as sincere disciples and with the respect befitting children, must venerate and honor in writing the spiritual Father, that is to say the Patriarch. He himself will likewise honor all his brothers and sons, the bishops. If it happens that a province resists, prompt and severe punishment will be inflicted on it by all the provinces; for if in their boldness they lay a hand against their leader, they will also dare to lay a hand against those who are beneath them.

Canon XV. — It has been said that, just as the Catholicos should not take the name of Patriarch until he had received the adhesion and imposition of the hands of the Metropolitans, the Metropolitan should not title metropolitan as long as he had not received the accession or ordination of the patriarch. And if membership is not given in accordance with the precepts laid down for this membership, but if something happens contrary to the canons, to the direction, to the statutes, to ecclesiastical tradition, we have defined, by the word of God. That the patriarch, the metropolitan or the bishop must be rejected and deposed from any rank of the priesthood.

Canon XVI. — It was said in the synod: "that sometimes, when for whatever reason the bishops of a province assemble near the head of the province for the examination of ecclesiastical affairs or to judge a person who has had the audacity to do anything contrary to ecclesiastical canons or to the general discipline of Christianity, this or that of the summoned bishops remains, does not come and does not send his adhesion; or, being present, leaves without giving his support to what all his clergy, the bishops of the province, are doing." — Concerning him, we have defined, by the word of God: "That having denounced the assembly of the bishops of the province, and having had the audacity to despise what the entire provincial assembly did, he must no longer be considered worthy of being summoned for common business. Furthermore, let him be banned from the metropolitan and the bishops of this province from any function of the priesthood. If he repents, devotes himself to penance, understands his fault, and presents a petition to all the bishops of the province so that they become his intercessors with the archbishop of this province. If he signs his sentence and confesses all his iniquity in writing, promising to change his conduct, and if, converting, he admits that he is rejected and removed from all orders of the priesthood, then he will be able to obtain mercy and forgiveness."

Canon XVII. — It was said in the assembly of bishops: "that a penalty proportionate to their rank should be imposed on those who commit fornication, so that the canons are not confused and no one judges matters that interest the community, recklessly, as the case may be, according to one's own will." — This is why we have defined, by the word of God, that: "If it is lay people who have committed fornication, they will be deprived of all ecclesiastical communion; if they understand their fault, if they do penance with good will and grieve, let the canons penitentially be applied to each according to their measure and as much as is sufficient. When the canon has received its fulfillment, then they will be allowed, through absolution, to participate in the communion of the Church. If he is a cleric, let the sentence be one year of fasting and prayer, and when he has completed the sentence, he will also be allowed to participate in ecclesiastical communion; — if he is a deacon, let his sentence be three years; — if it is a father who does not have a wife: seven years; and if it is a priest who has a wife, he will no longer be allowed to exercise the priesthood. — Likewise for bishops, according to the precepts of the synod of the Fathers. — No one is permitted to act otherwise."

Canon XVIII. — It was also said in the assembly of bishops when, in any province, the patriarch or the metropolitan of this province will have judged it appropriate, because of its extent and its development, the distance and its location. The separation of countries, urgent reasons which cause harm to ecclesiastical affairs, to constitute a new episcopal see, and to attribute to it jurisdiction over certain villages within the jurisdiction of neighboring sees, no one, apart from those who created it, cannot delete or cancel it. If bishops, in order to preserve their old boundaries, oppose the establishment of the see, in order not to lose the part of their diocese which must be annexed to the new see, let them be excommunicated and removed of the functions of the priesthood until they retract what they have said or attempted to do. It is indeed appropriate for true pastors to whom he has entrusted the rightful flock of Christ to pray and supplicate God at all times, and for any time so that their sheepfolds are preserved from all evil, to increase the quantity of their sheepfolds, to increase them and make them bear fruit. By this means, to increase the number of shepherds like them, so that at day of the resurrection they can cry to the supreme pastor: 'Lord, you have given us each five talents, behold we have brought back five talents each to them'; and let us say to them: 'Courage, good and faithful servants, you have been faithful in a little thing which has multiplied in your hands, enter into the joy of seeing the Master'."

Canon XIX. — He was further said: "that men who have received the gift of the Holy Spirit through holy baptism, who have participated in the holy mysteries, who have been accredited as familiars by the Christian fraternity, who have been instructed in the reading of the Holy Books, willingly devote

themselves to diabolical works, to pagan formulas of incantations, to ligatures, to amulets, to auguries, to divinations, or say that they
there are spirits, spells, horoscopes, or observe times and moments to carry out their actions. When one of those who have fallen into this great infirmity is converted, let him be offered as a means of healing, as to one who is physically ill, the oil of prayer, blessed by the priests, with the water of prayer, fasting, prayer, vigilance, continual vigils, until the cloud of foreign dust which enveloped him had left his mind. And that, moreover, we make him hear at all times the warning, the teaching, the blame, the reprimand which provide consolation, courage, hope and forgiveness. It is through this that one will be able to experience and know one's penance; and then, little by little, he will be admitted successively to some participations, but not all at once to the holy mysteries. If it is a priest, he will no longer be entrusted with the priestly ministry.

Canon XX. — It was forbidden by others that convents and martyrs should be built in towns or the surrounding areas of towns. Now, it was said in the assembly of bishops that this thought was contrary to Christianity, and that the pagans and the Jews rejoiced that Christianity was not developing and that the praise of God was not increasing. We therefore, according to the precepts of the Holy Books and according to the tradition which has spread and is current in the Holy Church, from the Blessed Apostles to this day, we strongly desire that churches, monasteries, temples be built, Martyria, in towns and the surrounding areas of towns. However, let the sacrifice not be offered there, and let the baptism not be confided there, except with the permission of the bishop and on certain days; the rest of the time they will receive communion from the main church, or it will be given constantly.

Canon XXI. — It was said in the assembly of the bishops of all the provinces that each would retain the honor of precedence over its neighbor, without anyone being allowed to introduce confusion or trouble to grow one or reduce the other. But each and every one of them, one after the other, will entirely keep each of their privileges according to the precept of the Holy Books, according to the canon of the synod of the Fathers, according to the tradition which is current and which exists in the holy Church of the western region and in Jotara. Unite the regions where Christianity flourishes and where the canons are observed. It is thus, in fact, that has become the Church, glorious bride, to be adorned with all beauties by her regularity, so that all those who see her praise in her the God Lord of all things. Anyone who revolts or rebels against these things will be rejected and removed from the rank he occupies, whatever it may be. — It also seemed good to the patriarch and to the assembly of his clergy the bishops, that, according to the tradition and paternal custom of the eastern region, observed until this day, when he who is patriarch dies, he to whom is entrusted to the episcopate of Katkar is to come without delay, as soon as he learns of it or is informed by letters, to the royal cities of Seleucia and Cteiphon, and, with the diligence which is incumbent on him more than all his clergy. The Jews of the patriarchal province, as being the second and the assistant of the patriarchal throne, he must address. Letters to the metropolitans and bishops of his clergy are to invite them to come, so that through them the election and ordination of the person who will be chosen for the patriarchate can be carried out. When he has learned or when someone has written to him about the event, if he delays and does not arrive after sufficient time, and if, after examination, the assembly of bishops judges that he has delayed without necessity, he has seemed good to the synod of bishops that he was deprived of all functions of his priesthood, until he came and received in the assembly the correction appropriate to his fault. He will no longer enjoy this prerogative, but he will be the last of all, instead of having the honor which had been attributed to him by the community, since he did not understand this goodness.

Canon XXII. — The assembly of bishops also wanted that the paternal canons which were renewed by the zeal of the catholicos Mar Aba, of good memory, be observed with care and that whoever transgresses them relives the punishment of his fault, according to it will seem suitable to the general assembly of bishops.

Canon XXIII. — The assembly of bishops also wanted that, when a deacon is prohibited by a priest, or a priest by his visitor, or a visitor by the chorbishop, or the chorbishop by him the bishop, or the bishop by the metropolitan, or the metropolitan by the patriarch, then even if one would say that he who has been forbidden has done so without just reason, the prohibition be observed with care. He who is forbidden will remain under censure and will ask to be judged in a general assembly before those who are of a higher rank than the one who censured and the one who was censured. When the matter has been examined by the assembly, their proceedings will receive a solution according to what justice will prescribe.

COUNCIL OF SELEUCIA-CTESIPHON

This synod was confirmed by the signatures and seals of the holy friends of God:
1. Mar Joseph, bishop, Catholicos
2. Mar Simeon, bishop, Metropolitan of Beit Houzoyi
3. Mar Paulus, bishop, Metropolitan of Nisibus
4. Mar Mesabbeha, bishop, Metropolitan of Hedayab
5. Mar Claudianus, bishop, Metropolitan of Mahozi-Hedata
6. Soubhalmaran, bishop of Kaikar
7. Simeon, bishop of Peroz-Sabour
8. Acacius, bishop of Madai
9. Yonannan, bishop of BeitDmraye
10. Bar Noun, bishop of Karmi
11. Denna , bishop of Masabadan
12. Abraham, bishop of Ispahan
13. Yezdegerd, bishop of Balad
14. Yzedpanan, bishop of Ma'alta
15. Ahoudemmen bishop of Ninive
16. Narse, bishop of Mahozw-Arewan;
17. Tahmin, bishop of Siarzoar
18. Yobanann, bishop of Abeward and of Sahr-Peroz

And of those who have adhered to the letter with their own seal:

19. Mar David, bishop, Metropolitan of Merse
20. Pousai, bishop of Holwan
21. Sourin, bishop of Karka Ledan
22. Sila, bishop of Hormizd-Ardasir
23. Elisee, bishop of Soustere
24. Kosrau, bishop of Sous
25. Bar Cauma, bishop of Qardou
26. Natoum, bishop of Arzdn of Beit Aoustan

And later came the accession of: Alahazeka, metropolitan of Beit Garmai

And the commemoration of Mar Johanan, metropolitan of Pherat-Maisan, was late in arriving. He retained his place in third row. Because the first metropolitan is that from Beit Houzaye; the second, that of Nisibis; the third soul, that of Pherat; the fourth, that of Hedayab; the fifth that of Beit Garmai; the sixth, that of Rew-Ardaftir; the seventh, that of Merw. At the head of all is the patriarch who sits on the Catholic throne of Seleucia and Ctesiphon. He is the Father and head of all metropolitans which are begotten by his laying on of hands and his authority; and any metropolitan who was established without him must be totally disposed and dismissed.

The Scriptorium Project is the work of a small group of lay people of various apostolic churches who are interested in the preservation, transmission, and translation of the works of the early and medieval church. Our efforts are to make the works of the church fathers accessible to anyone who might have an interest in Christian antiquities and the theological, philosophical, and moral writings that have become the bedrock of Western Civilization.

To-date, our releases have pulled from the Greek, Syriac, Georgian, Latin, Celtic, Ethiopian, and Coptic traditions of Christianity, and have been pulled from sundry local traditions and languages.

Other Works of the Ancient Persian and Indian Church Series:

Council of Seleucia-Ctesiphon: Under Mar Joseph 554 AD by Mar Joseph of Seleucia (June 2014)
Council of Seleucia-Ctesiphon: Under Mar Yahbalaha 420 AD by Yahbalaha of Seleucia (Aug 2015)
Council of Seleucia-Ctesiphon: Under Mar Dadisho 424 AD by Mar Dadisho of Seleucia (Sept. 2016)
The Ramban Pattukal: the song of St. Thomas in Kerala by Ramban the Archdeacon (May 2017)
The Acts of St. Thomas in India (June 2018)
Council of Seleucia-Ctesiphon: Under Mar Babai 497 AD by Mar Babai of Seleucia (Feb. 2021)
Council of Seleucia-Ctesiphon: Under Mar Isaac 410 AD by Isaac of Seleucia (May 2021)
Council of Seleucia-Ctesiphon: Under Mar Aba I 544 AD by Aba I of Seleucia (July 2021)

www.ingramcontent.com/pod-product-compliance
Lightning Source LLC
LaVergne TN
LVHW051924060526
838201LV00060B/4163